Grow It Back!

Diana Noonan

Contents

Hair

You have hair.
It can be cut.

Your hair will
grow back!

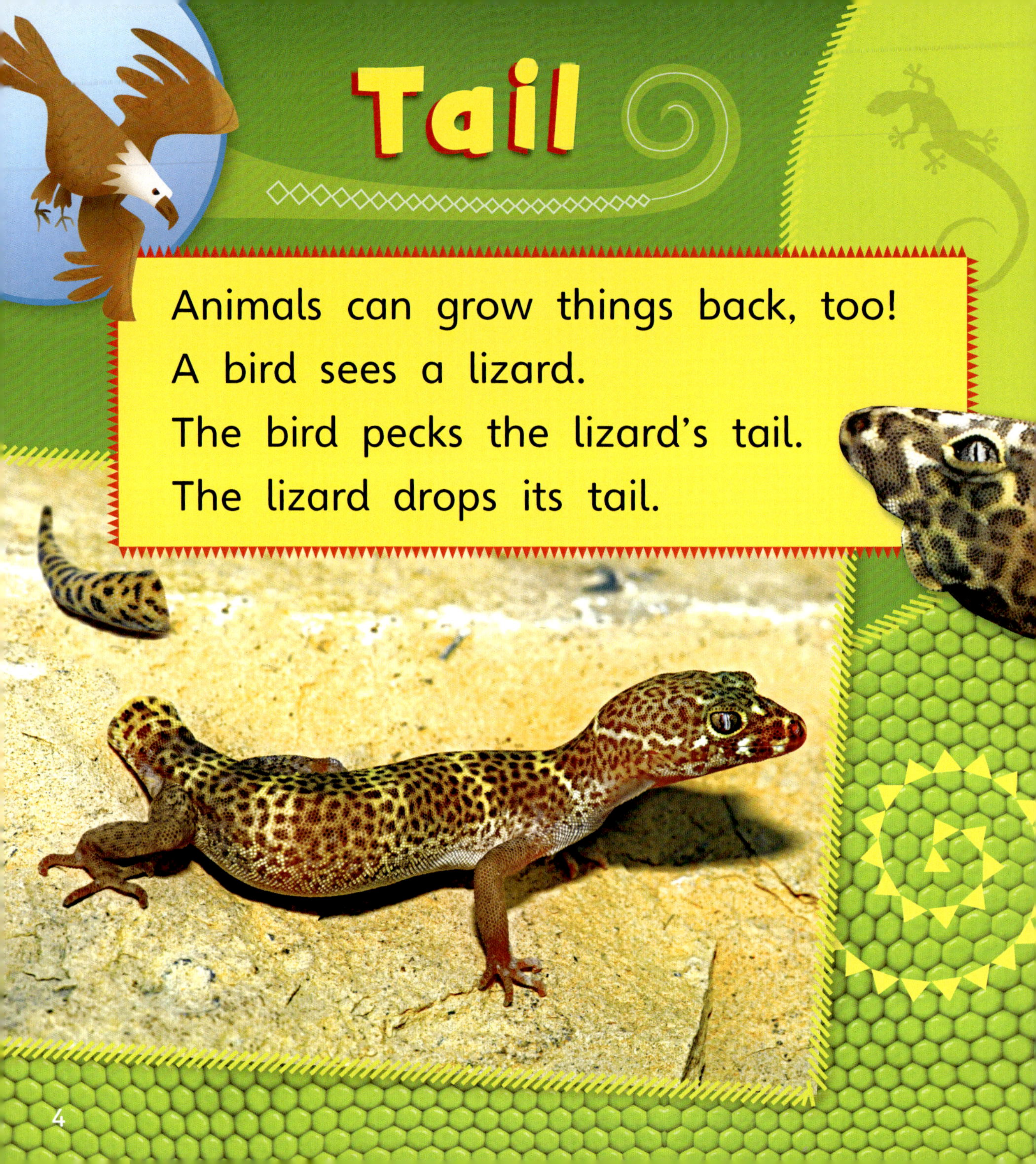

Tail

Animals can grow things back, too!
A bird sees a lizard.
The bird pecks the lizard's tail.
The lizard drops its tail.

The lizard runs away.
The tail will grow back.

Arm

A bird sees a starfish.
The bird pecks at the starfish.

The arm of the starfish comes off. The arm will grow back.

Leg

A bird sees a stick insect.
The bird pecks the insect's leg.

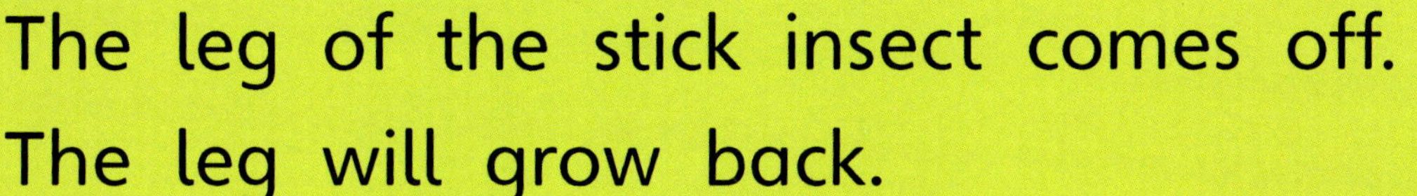

The leg of the stick insect comes off.
The leg will grow back.

A new leg is growing here.

Claw

A bird sees a crab.
The bird pecks at the crab's claw.
The claw comes off.

The claw will grow back.

Antlers

The deer have a fight.
Their antlers hit.

An antler comes off.
The antler will grow back.

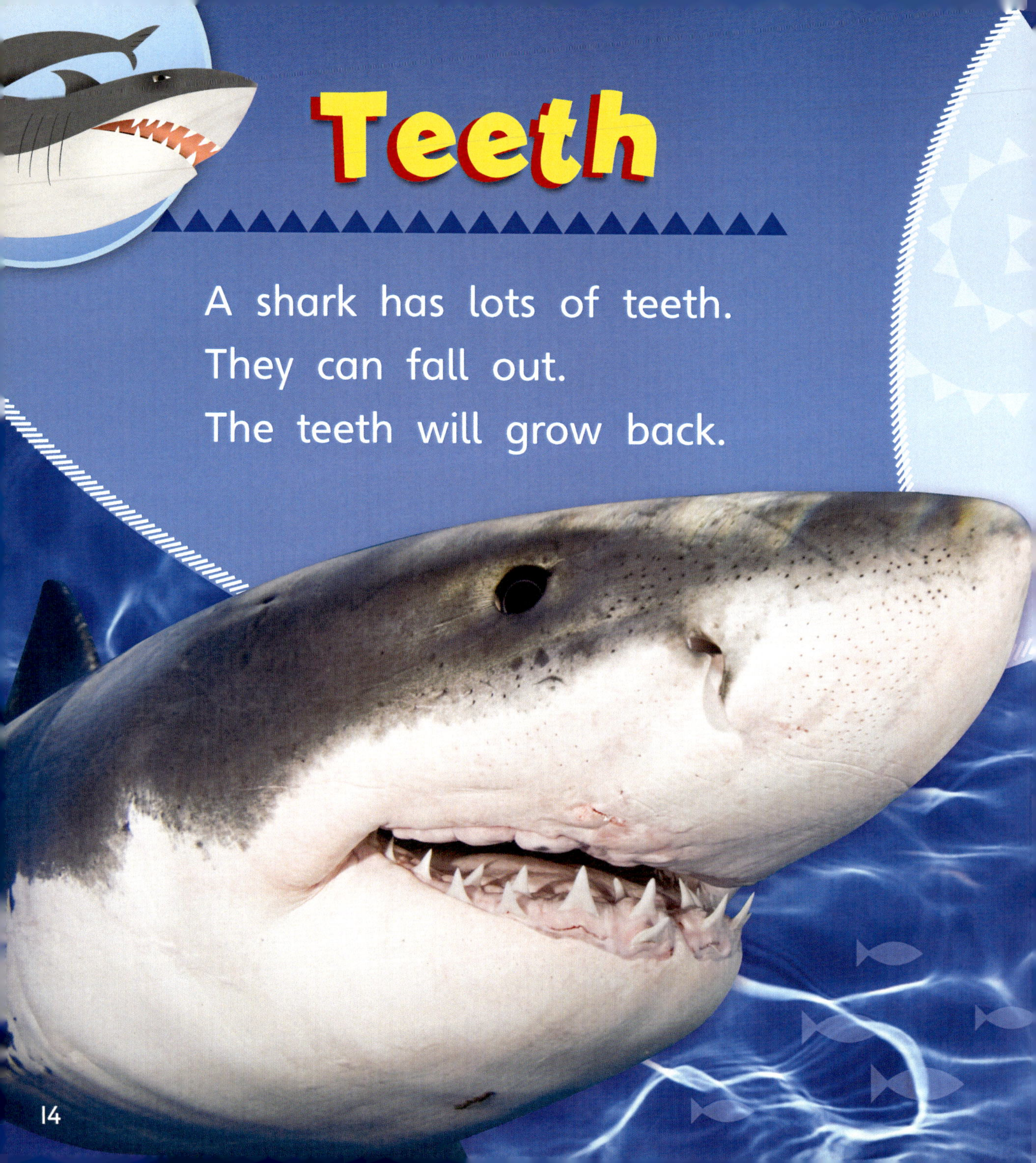

Teeth

A shark has lots of teeth.
They can fall out.
The teeth will grow back.

You have lots of little teeth.
They will fall out.
You will grow **new** teeth!

Index